W9-BAT-446

LET'S see

Election Day

by Marc Tyler Nobleman

Content Adviser: Heidi Pendergast, Voter Registration Coordinator,
Rock The Vote, Los Angeles, California

Reading Adviser: Susan Kesselring, M.A., Literacy Educator,
Rosemount-Apple Valley-Eagan (Minnesota) School District

Let's See Library
Compass Point Books
Minneapolis, Minnesota

Compass Point Books
3109 West 50th Street, #115
Minneapolis, MN 55410

Visit Compass Point Books on the Internet at *www.compasspointbooks.com*
or e-mail your request to *custserv@compasspointbooks.com*

On the cover: A political button

Photographs ©:William Whitehurst/Corbis, cover; Bradley C. Bower-Pool/Getty Images, 4; Michael Springer/Getty
Images, 6; David Butow/Corbis SABA, 8; North Wind Picture Archives, 10, 16; Library of Congress, 12; Bruce Coleman
Inc./Debra P. Hershkowitz, 14; Fort Lauderdale Sentinel/Corbis SYGMA, 18; Spencer Platt/Getty Images, 20.

Creative Director: Terri Foley
Managing Editor: Catherine Neitge
Editors: Brenda Haugen and Christianne Jones
Photo Researcher: Marcie C. Spence
Designers: Melissa Kes and Les Tranby
Educational Consultant: Diane Smolinski

Library of Congress Cataloging-in-Publication Data
Nobleman, Marc Tyler.
    Election day / by Marc Tyler Nobleman.
        v. cm.—(Let's see)
    Includes bibliographical references and index.
    Contents: What is election day?—Why is election day on a Tuesday?—Why is election day in November?—
What happens on election day?—How do people vote on election day?—Who can vote and who can run for
President on election day?—Have all Americans always had the right to vote?—Are there any problems with
election day?—What does election day mean to people?—Glossary—Did you know?—Want to know more?
ISBN 0-7565-0644-1
1. Elections–United States–History–Juvenile literature. 2. Election Day–History–Juvenile literature.
[1. Elections. 2. Election Day–History.] I. Title. II. Series.
    JK1978.N63 2004
    324.6'0973 —dc22   2003022178

Table of Contents

What Is Election Day? 5

What Happens on Election Day? 7

How Do People Vote? 9

Why Is Election Day on a Tuesday? 11

Why Is Election Day in November? 13

Who Can Vote and Who Can Run for President? 15

Have All Americans Always Had the Right to Vote? 17

Are There Any Problems with Election Day? 19

What Does Election Day Mean to People? 21

Glossary 22
Did You Know?...22
Want to Know More? 23
Index 24

NOTE: In this book, words that are defined in the glossary
are in **bold** the first time they appear in the text.

What Is Election Day?

Election Day is when people vote. They choose the people they want to lead their cities, states, and country. The people trying to get **elected** are called **candidates**.

A candidate who is elected **represents** everyone in his or her area. Once elected, the person's job is to listen to what the people want and improve the government to make people's lives better.

In the United States, Election Day is set by law. It is always the Tuesday after the first Monday in November in even-numbered years. Even-numbered years end in a 0, 2, 4, 6, or 8. Elections for president happen every four years.

◀ *John F. Street campaigns to be reelected as mayor of Philadelphia.*

What Happens on Election Day?

In the United States, most people vote at the nearest **polling place**. The polling place may be a fire station, church, school, or some other building.

People vote by secret **ballot**. Those who can't come to a polling place can vote by **absentee ballot**. They mail in their absentee ballots after they fill them out. In most states, absentee ballots must arrive back at the election office by Election Day.

The polling places close in the evening. Then the votes are counted. Most people find out who won the elections by listening to or reading news reports.

◄ *North Carolina Senator John Edwards and his wife, Elizabeth, read the paper.*

How Do People Vote?

There are many ways to vote, but all the types of voting are private. Most people make their choices in voting booths. Then machines count the votes.

One way of voting is by using a punch card. Voters punch holes in cards next to the names of the candidates they want to choose.

Some vote using a special machine with a lever. Voters move the levers next to the names of the candidates they choose. Another way of voting is **optical scan voting**. People make dark marks on cards next to their candidates' names.

Some states use electronic voting. Voters touch screens or push buttons to make choices.

◀ *People vote in a San Francisco fire station.*

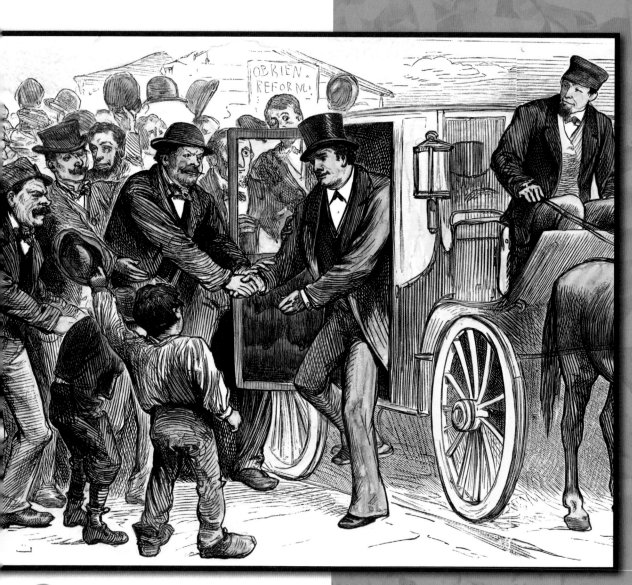

Why Is Election Day on a Tuesday?

In 1845, the U.S. government made the law saying when each Election Day would be. Election Day was set on a Tuesday to give voters enough time to get to the **polls**. At the time, people had to walk or ride horses on rocky dirt roads to get to where they voted. Some people needed more than one day to get to the nearest polling place.

Most people would not leave their towns on a Sunday because they went to church. People could leave on a Monday. So the government chose Tuesday for Election Day. That gave people plenty of time to travel to vote.

◀ *A candidate visits the polls in the 1800s.*

Why Is Election Day in November?

The United States is a **democracy.** In a democracy, citizens have the right to vote for their leaders. It is important that all citizens get a chance to vote.

At the time the Election Day law was made, most Americans were farmers. Election Day was put in November because farmers were not as busy then as they were the rest of the year. Farmers planted crops in spring and summer. Most gathered their crops in September or October.

In winter, the cold, wet weather in parts of the country made travel difficult. The weather in early November was usually nice enough for travel. So early November was the best time for Election Day.

◄ *Farmers worked in the fields until late autumn.*

DONNA SHARP
For State Committee

Register to Vote

FOR A SAFER
AND MORE
LIVABLE
NEW YORK

DONATIONS

Who Can Vote and Who Can Run for President?

On Election Day, all people who meet the **requirements** can vote. In most states, people must register, or get on the official list to vote. A person registers by filling out a form found at libraries, post offices, or even online.

Voters must be U.S. citizens and be at least 18 years old. Citizens are people who were born in a country or have the right to live there. Voters must live in the state in which they vote.

To run for president, a person must have been born in the United States. Candidates for president also have to be at least 35 years old.

◀ *A woman fills out a form so she can vote.*

Have All Americans Always Had the Right to Vote?

For a long time, many Americans were not allowed to vote. Each state decided who could vote there. Often, only white men who owned land could vote. In most states, women, blacks, Native Americans, and others were not allowed to vote.

By the mid-1800s, white men who did not own land got the right to vote. In 1870, a law called the 15th Amendment to the **Constitution** gave all men the right to vote, not just white men. Fifty years later, the 19th Amendment was passed. This law said women could vote. The Indian Citizenship Act of 1924 let Native Americans vote, too.

◄ *Women march in 1911 in the hope of earning the right to vote.*

Are There Any Problems with Election Day?

Election Day is important, but it is not a holiday in most states. Many people have to work on Election Day. Some people find it hard to leave work to vote. Many polling places open early or stay open late so people can vote before or after work.

In the United States, voter **turnout** is often low. Some people choose not to vote because they are not interested. Some forget to register in time. Others think their votes don't make a difference. The truth is every vote counts.

◀ *Some people line up to vote before going to work or taking their children to school.*

What Does Election Day Mean to People?

Election Day reminds people they help make their government work. Voters have a big job on Election Day. They get to choose who will be the leaders in their cities, states, and country.

In some countries, people are not allowed to vote. Americans know it is a **privilege** to vote.

Candidates show voters they want to help make things better for everyone. On Election Day, voters show candidates they care about the future. If people are not happy with their government, they can change it on Election Day.

◀ *People in New York who voted for George Pataki for governor celebrate his win.*

Glossary

absentee ballot—a vote that is sent to the election office by mail because the voter can't go to the polling place on Election Day

ballot—a vote

candidate—a person who wants to be chosen as a leader in an election

Constitution—the document stating the basic laws of the United States

democracy—a form of government in which people choose their leaders by voting

elected—chosen for a job by a vote

optical scan voting—a way to vote; a voter makes dark marks on a card, and a machine reads, or scans, those marks

polling place—a place where people vote

polls—special places where people go to vote

privilege—a special right or advantage

represents—to speak or act for someone else

requirements—something you need to have or do

turnout—the number of people who vote

Did You Know?

❋ On Election Day, schools are closed in some states, including Delaware, Hawaii, Illinois, Rhode Island, South Carolina, and West Virginia.

❋ So far, each U.S. president has been a white male. However, anyone who meets the requirements can run for president. One day, Americans might elect a president who is female, black, Hispanic, or from any other background.

❋ At one time, most states said people had to be at least 21 years old to vote. In 1971, the 26th Amendment lowered the voting age to 18 everywhere in the United States.

❋ Even after the 15th Amendment was passed, some white people still would not let black men vote. The 1965 Voting Rights Act was a law that helped make sure people couldn't be stopped from voting because of the color of their skin.

Want to Know More?

In the Library

Christelow, Eileen. *Vote!* New York: Clarion Books, 2003.

Raatma, Lucia. *Susan B. Anthony.* Minneapolis: Compass Point Books, 2001.

Rustad, Martha E. H. *Susan B. Anthony.* Mankato, Minn.: Capstone Press, 2002.

Wooldridge, Connie Nordhielm. *When Esther Morris Headed West: Women, Wyoming, and the Right to Vote.* New York: Holiday House, 2001.

On the Web

For more information on *Election Day,* use FactHound to track down Web sites related to this book.

1. Go to *http://www.facthound.com*
2. Type in a search word related to this book or this book ID: 0756506441.
3. Click on the *Fetch It* button.

Your trusty FactHound will fetch the best Web sites for you!

On the Road

National Voting Rights Museum & Institute
1012 Water Ave.
Selma, Ala. 36701
334/418-0800
To learn more about the history of voting in the United States

Index

absentee ballots, 7
amendments, 17
ballots, 7
blacks, 17
candidates, 5, 9, 15, 21
Constitution, 17
date, 5, 11, 13
democracy, 13
electronic voting, 9
farmers, 13
15th Amendment, 17
government, 5, 11, 21
Indian Citizenship Act, 17
machines, 9
Native Americans, 17

19th Amendment, 17
November, 5, 13
optical scan voting, 9
polling places, 7, 11, 19
presidential elections, 5, 15
punch cards, 9
registration, 15, 19
requirements, 15
voter registration, 15, 19
voter turnout, 19
voting, 5, 7, 9, 21
voting booths, 9
voting requirements, 15
voting rights, 17
women, 17

About the Author

Marc Tyler Nobleman has written more than 40 books for young readers. He has also written for a History Channel show called "The Great American History Quiz" and for several children's magazines including *Nickelodeon, Highlights for Children,* and *Read* (a Weekly Reader publication). He is also a cartoonist, and his single panels have appeared in more than 100 magazines internationally. He lives in Connecticut.